leadbelly

The National Poetry Series was established in 1978 to ensure the publication of five poetry books annually through participating publishers. Publication is funded by the Lannan Foundation; the late James A. Michener and Edward J. Piszek through the Copernicus Society of America; Stephen Graham; International Institute of Modern Letters; Joyce & Seward Johnson Foundation; Juliet Lea Hillman Simonds Foundation; and the Tiny Tiger Foundation. This project is also supported in part by an award from the National Endowment for the Arts, which believes that a great nation deserves great art.

2004 Competition Winners

David Friedman of New York, New York, *The Welcome*
Chosen by Stephen Dunn, published by University of Illinois Press

Tyehimba Jess of Brooklyn, New York, *leadbelly*
Chosen by Brigit Pegeen Kelly, published by Verse Press

Corinne Lee of Austin, Texas, *PYX*
Chosen by Pattiann Rogers, published by Penguin Books

Ange Mlinko of Brooklyn, New York, *Starred Wire*
Chosen by Bob Holman, published by Coffee House Press

Camille Norton of Stockton, California, *Corruption*
Chosen by Campbell McGrath, published by HarperCollins

NATIONAL
ENDOWMENT
FOR THE ARTS

leadbelly
TYEHIMBA JESS

The National Poetry Series Selected by Brigit Pegeen Kelly

Verse Press • Amherst, MA

Published by Verse Press

Verse Press titles are distributed to the trade by Consortium Book Sales
and Distribution, 1045 Westgate Drive, St. Paul, Minnesota 55114.

Library of Congress Cataloging-in-Publication Data:

Jess, Tyehimba.
  Leadbelly : poems / Tyehimba Jess.— 1st ed.
      p. cm. — (National poetry series)
  Includes bibliographical references.
  ISBN-13: 978-0-9746353-3-0 (pbk. : alk. paper)
  ISBN-10: 0-9746353-3-2 (pbk. : alk. paper)
  1. Leadbelly, 1885-1949—Poetry. 2. African American
musicians—Poetry. 3. Blues musicians—Poetry.
  4. Blues (Music)—Poetry. I. Title. II. Series.
  PS3610.E874L43 2005
  811'.6—dc22

    2005007247

Cover Art: Krista Franklin, "leadbelly." Used by permission of the artist.
Design and composition by J. Johnson.

Printed in the United States of America

9 8 7 6 5 4 3 2 1

First Edition

contents

good morning babe, how do you do?

leadbelly's lessons

mr. haney owned
shreveport's general store
where a dollar a week
bought my 12 year old frame's
lift and lunge of barrel and crate
across a sawdust floor.
still, he wanted more.

the guitar refused to get naked
with haney. he would fumble
up the seams of its hidden croon;
hook, clasp and bodice of each tune
mangled down to a stunted strum. so,

he'd quit. he'd hoist bourbon
and order me to hoist song,
the velvet locomotive of marrow deep hum
i'd tote up from the swollen center of guitar,
its catch and slide caught between palms
and cradled 'cross louisiana starlight.

his bottle and scowl grew louder
with each reel and jump that i played
while getting paid to show the way
of undressing music from its wooden clothes.

but it was like coaxin' stone
to bathe in sky. he never let his flesh
wallow in the blue floatin' 'round his earth,
so he buried himself deeper in his own dirt.
he'd think on the hurt a white man can do
without second thought—he'd slur
nigger, someday i'm gonna kill you.
and stagger home.

it was there, alone,
in the dark, darkness of me
that i first learned the ways
of pure white envy.

and thank you, mr. haney,
for teaching me...

what kind of soul has man?

sallie ledbetter: a mother's hymn

when the black boy climbs out of my womb:

how to peel dynamite from his bones?

how to strip tornado's hum from his ears?

how to weed graveyard from his garden of tongue?

what rainbow of prayer to pull between teeth?

how to blind him from liquor's sun of stupor?

how to sow whisper into his hurricane of hips?

what blizzard of plea to freeze his tremor of feet?

how to lift him from streetlight blaze?

which revengeful breast fed him this poison?

which breast gilded his mouth with song?

john wesley ledbetter

singing a crusade of axe and machete, i take virgin texas territory by force, clear it of timber and trouble. each eastern twilight, i till top soil 'til sun plants itself back into that western horizon. i keep struggling against a brooding moon's skyline until dark sleep is my friend again, a place where i can dream drought into rain, pray storm cloud out of spotless sky.

i pick cotton like a desperate thief hunting copper pennies hidden beneath each lock of boll. there's only one way out of slave time dues: hump this land down till it shrieks up a crop of cancelled debt into your wagon, works its water-into-wine magic that conjures me from sharecropping servant to citizenship.

my surviving son is the harvest of starlit sweat soaked hours stolen from a greedy 70 acre mistress and plowed between sallie's slung back legs. when i first hold him, a sun bronzed seed sprung from black cherokee womb, i know for the first time a weight that lifts me high above soil.

colt protection special

his daddy brings him to me
fresh and fifteen, a boy beggin'
to know me like a virgin
wind risin' to fuck a hurricane.

while his fist cloaks me
with the hush of broken youth,
i singe my bullet-toothed birth–
right into his fingertips. he hefts
my black powdered blue steel
mass, aims high to heaven,
wonders how easy it is to slip
into god's dirty clothes.

fannin street signifies

i shake the dust off farm boys' heels,
pound their pulse with dice and delirium,
suckle them to swagger with alley-
hard nipples spouting 100 proof
rumors of gap-thighed awe.

i give them what they want
till their swollen chested dreams snap,
spill crimson at the seams.

this one rushes at me like a blade
out of darkness, seeking glory's
keloid rise across my gutter ripe skin.

fine.

i cut a hole in his heart,
nail in a dozen metronomes,
each timed to the rhythm
of a newfound sinner's sigh.

i line his throat with a church-
load of moonlight, smear blues' afterbirth
of bible and baal across his skull.

i stuff his ears with 1000 bales
of barrelhouse folklore,
plant his tongue in the cunt of song.

mistress stella speaks

you think i'm his property
'cause he paid cash
to grab me by the neck,
swing me 'cross his knee
and stroke the living song from my hips.

you think he is master of all
my twelve tongues, spreading notes
thick as a starless night, strangling spine
till my voice is a jungle of chords.

the truth is that i owned him
since the word *love* first blessed his lips
since *hurt* and *flight* and *free*
carved their way into the cotton
fused bones of his fretting hand,
since he learned how pleading men hunt
for my face in the well of their throats
till their tongues are soaked with want.

yes, each day he comes back
home from the fields,
from chain gang fury,
from the smell of sometime women
who borrow his body. he bends
his weight around me
like a wilting weed,
drinking in my kiss
of fretboard across fingertip
'til he can stand up straight again,
aching from what he left behind,
rising sure as dawn.

1912: blind lemon jefferson explaining to leadbelly

…an' everything gotta be 'live on you son. read the crowd like a fortune teller's tealeaf, from the *plunk* of a nickel to the *bang* of a quarter to the smell of thieves schemin' on a blind man's cash.

see this scar? i was between guitars in san antonio and broke enough to wrestle men for carnival money. the one that did this had come back three times for a ass whuppin' only a fool could want again, but when he pulled that shiv outta his boot, didn't nobody say nothin'—had they bets on how hard i was gonna bleed. that's what the world is, son. desperate enough to pin a blind man's back to the ground for all the money he can't never even see. hungry enough to chop him down for takin' what he's earned. that's what the world is. they lost money that day. an' i squeezed my stella out the pawnbroker's grip one last time.

that's what that box o' strings is, son. your boxcar ticket outta nowhere. maybe even steak dinner, silk ties, and all the leg you can stroke. but you gotta wrestle for it, son. you *got* to…

what you gonna do
when the world's on fire?

caddo born

i am a lake caddo man, born from texarkana dust, where boll
weevil stows a worried harvest in our cotton sacks, and the
nearest white face may be twenty miles away. i want the world in
my char black hands: and this starvation box with strings beats a
blindin' rhythm past cotton fields and the horses i break between
my knees. this wooden head with open mouth i caress and thrash
will shake down the swollen tree of money and women where i
kneel like a little boy in sunday school.

give me daddy's pistol and a fresh work song. let me spread this
fever from breakdown to uptown fannin street of shreveport,
where the red river snakes its hoodoo into my fingers that snap
wire and wood, where sukey jumps blur into a midnight that
peels the tin roof off the sky.

blind lemon taught me

i remember a useless eyed street busker, twin holes shriveled small behind smoked spectacles. the parables he taught in the troubled space between each note. sometimes, i would close my eyes, run my fingers through landscape where he'd placed his hands to solve the riddle of my features, his fingertips supple winged blackbirds. fluttering from brow to eyelash to cheek to chin, he found my true face, stretched those knuckle jointed roots from ebony trunk of wrist and ashen palm to grow as one with the wood of his twelve string. there, he told how a man can trade pieces of himself for a song. an eye here, an ankle there, a ball if he's not careful, and the fret board's friction that turns silken skin to callus. i remember how he bottlenecked blues caught between the teeth of each tin pan alley tune, nailed it in a patent leather stomp, moved streetcorner crowds down another mile of his train tracked voice with every beat. i remember how every song stitched together my story, how he took something away when he discovered my face beneath his palms, gave it back on layaway plan of bent notes, bloodied moons.

misfire

when jake carter's scotch and whiskey hands came too close to the music growling its way out of my baby's hip, i told him slow behind a clenched excuse for smile that them watermelon hips and sundown lips was mine for dinner that night. but some men don't listen 'til heaven's tidal wave swallows 'em whole, spits them up into a slaughterhouse noose.

the .32 colt kicked hot into my grip, snarled its way level with the head of a man who refused to take death seriously. i tackled him hard, cocked back the hammer, but i only recall the empty shutter snap that froze him dead for a shell-shocked heartbeat, then released, filled him full of lazarus. left me with only a gun butt to blast him into black and blue sleep.

harris county chain gang

they trial me. truss me. trade me downriver for a book full of words that spells out my month-long sentence. they want to shrink my castle of will down to outhouse stink. they want me to reek of crapped out snake eyes and deathbed moan.

they want me to forget me. to forget i am flesh. i am one. we, black forever of bent shoulder, bowed head, bonded voice swinging a cemeteried freight of penitentiary chain. we steady thud of wind with lungs that empty moon, fill it back up with shine, feed my feet to pig iron anklets biting flesh where i am chain. i am flesh. i am link. i will break. bleed, crack. shatter. crush.

i'ma smash outta this choir, come up gasping new breath, my name burned clean, made mine.

alias: walter boyd

my conception a crime, my birth a necessity, i was born pregnant
with possibility. did my bowie-county-sharecropper-best to drag
him to redemption. swore off women and wine like they was
kissin' cousin to the songsterizin' strapped and muzzled in the
back of my brain. saved my sweat for choirs and sermons, testified
a sacrament of would-be salvation.

i confess. the fat black hand of twelve string clamor pulled me
slow off my pulpit of humble. swapped the dry psalms stuffed
in my mouth for cool cigar smoke of dirty dozen slurs. his eyes
burrowed their way back inside my head, his wildflower fingers
curled their way around another moonshine mistress' knees, and
there i smothered between the laughing thighs of nigger drunk
dreams.

lethe on leadbelly

once, towards the end,
sun burned her face into my back
as i rode him raw between our cotton rows,
wearing his skin into the boll's hungry bed
as if i could bury the low mosquito hum
of perfumed women clinging to his sweat.

i had wanted him for myself, alone.
followed him from fannin street to convict row.
when prison's pig iron fist couldn't hold him down
i ran in his tracks to bowie county, where we planted
a new name into soil that strained us thin
till convict stripes called his name again.

once, towards the end,
sun whipped her laughter onto my back
until i rode myself free,
and when we were done
we were done for good.
and all i could smell
was the cotton,
myself,
the road.

the blood done signed your name

for trouble's sake

take hips firmer than fatback, a mouth that peels the color red raw between its lips, the jutted angle of juju in her breasts, and there you have chammie. add two caddo men, a full moon, a .32, and what you have left is my story. add prison farm and time, subtract lawyer fees that steal my daddy's land. shrink wealth down to just another sharecropped dream, and rub it in my skin each morning with salt of the straw boss' call. here i am, at the end of each cipher, nothin' but a dirty brown hum to stretch between my fingers, nothin' but whip seared air to hold my song. here i am, in sugarland.

bud russel, louisiana prison transfer man, 1920

leadbelly you say.
killer   huh.
singer   huh.

look.

i herd them   gang by gang
moaning and dumb   cross country
to wherever   steel needs hands.
and there were there are   so many.
enough to fill cotton fields   with hands

you say he sang   played guitar.
seems like all of em   had a tune
buried under they breath   a itch
what ain't been   beat out of em
yet.
          that is my work:
a kinda talent   to smell trouble
with a knife   and cut.

twelve-string   huh.
howler   huh.

let me tell you something.
they's all howlin'.
they a crop of twisted wind.
they was   they is like   a harvest

i reap.

father

daddy comes to prison, hands empty of acreage and ownership, the price he pays for my crash of cold nerve and craze that flowed a river of will stafford's blood at my feet. my father comes in june, clutching the sum of his life under penitent palms, cash on the counter for my prodigal hide. my father comes, on stilted legs of age, his hands blistered prayers holding greenbacked promises, a negotiation waiting to happen when he sees the warden, unleashes the stones in his voice to beg my pardon's price. my father comes dying, body of bent birch whispering all my youth's secrets, his steady climb onto each morning's sunrisen shoulders from our farm's horizon as he cleared each acre of pine to shove cotton's white face from soil through fingers dirty with sharecropped dream. he stands before me, slammed down to this, his stare into the numbers striping 'cross my chest as he tells me how no price can buy my freedom. my father comes to barbed wire mesh of my home, tells me how time has wrapped its fist around his skull, shut itself tight in the moment before numbered days and weeks unravel themselves, release him back to dust and gravel he no longer owns. in november, he is gone.

leadbelly: runagate

where water and land meet is shore, and on shore is iron in fists of jailers in sun of texas swamp. i wade into bubble and blue ink of red river, my head a shaven, bobbing, brown island of shine. a warden's finger etches the balance of my life on the trigger, weighs up the finance of lead vs. nigger labor, as he yells one last time for my life. and here we all are, stuck in this crossroads hard as the bullet i hammered into a man's heart in bowie county.

let the hound come, ol' rattler ripping jaws into my flesh, while i wade this brazos baptism of blood and water. i know it's over, there will be no more chase today, and so what do i have left between this hellhound's jaws and freedom's crucifixion in the hell of sugarland? i let the canine neck snap under my sickle of fingers, my blessing, this sacrament of water.

i want to let the water take me, i want to surrender to this river's rock and swirl, come up clean and white as death itself, but the black in me breaks down into blues, and now i feel the coffle of their claws. i am stepping toward dry land, the dance of ankle chains, where i scream history into song that works itself into blood, sweat, memory.

leadbelly: from sugarland

i push groan from gut, birthing a bloodlight into song, black wave of texas roil rippin' cross cane field, heat mirage of field holler syncopation, missin' link in a chain of gospel moans. i stand here gideon sung, swinging sickle across cane where i record the roadmap of pain, the way this confection bends my back to a blood brown halo of motion, fills my grip with blistered flesh, twists the sun into high noon heat from dawn 'til dusk. every day marches crushed and crippled into sin sugared misery, bottom lands blessed with our sweltered hymn curse.

i will tell you now and only once: only one way out. past bloodhound and 20:20 gunshot, past swamp and gator tooth, past lynch rope and lash: work these muthafuckas down. outsweat and outshine even the hardest cracker smile, 'til they think you death's scarecrow, 'til your grin tilts itself into their daydreams, and your field holler moves the white chalked nerve in them to wonder black, pauses, tells them the truth in the lie they wanna hear: how you is more a man than they ever wet dreamed to be, how your voice carves the bludgeon of legend into a bent down sound that sways up earth. how one black sound can tremble down these walls, how i'll pick up each and every one of the twelve humming strings and make a chorus of auction blocks and mama wails, how the midnight special cries for me in a single streak of smoke headed north.

sing   out

"I am going to turn you loose after a while, but I'm going to keep you here so you can pick and dance for me a while."
　　　　　　　　　　　　　　—Texas Governor Pat Neff

he came here a pharaoh, his caravan of coupes swarming our convict campground, carrying good whiskey and good time women that stared us up from every corner of their eyes. they use me for their muscle bound box of juke, their porch monkey swing with tension and tune crammed into fingertip. i beat this stringed–up beggar's bowl, grip this neck, grit and grace a potion i layer into each footstomp. each lyric and grin sings redemption, each chord smuggles rage and roar through telegraph wires of this 12 string sound.

ol stack o' dollars seals his voice around the music firm as a handcuff, and i pick the lock on stella's strings to open a doorway in this white man's mind, a place i will crawl, leap, shuck and jive my way through any way i can, long as the other side has a one way train ticket waitin' for me like my lethe's open legs. with sunset, i claim the wooden bandstand alone and let it loose, proverb and plea and prayer all pulled into one song from my open open mouth. one by one i hear the tumblers of his mind click in my hand, twisting under weight of my shuffle and shine. i stick my black hand in his heart and squeeze the bloodless chamber for one last drop of juice as the breakdown grinds to numb silence.

Governor Pat Neff
August 25, 1924

Dear Yu Honor
Yu may rmember me when yu visits prison
here I am Walter Boyd Leadbelly #42738
yo best big niger from Sugarland Farm
wit my stella guitar and songs yu like
I play it all like a black machine for yu loud an slow
Down in the valley   What a frend we have in
Jesus an I Sugarland shuffle like pickin cotton far as
eye cn see I need my freedom like yu said yu was gone give me
yur honor all I need a second chance rmembr me
yu sed I was som niger   som niger need they pardon
GOVERNOR
thank yu for yo kind kind hand yo wisdum.

freedom

freedom is what you can buy with a song. after the song has been soldered into your lungs. after the song has beaten its way inside your dreams. after the song has snuck its way into your bed. after the song has festered and blossomed and festered again. after the song has stolen your fingers and robbed your voice blind. after all this, you try to sell the song that can never be sold. you end up with your hand out, waiting for the words that spell freedom.

freedom is every dirt road ground into whiskey still of my voice, my backpocket buck knife sharpening silence, coiled up close to copperhead, dime and dollar bill, the price of a pint and the slow violence of a victrola spittin' bessie's blues. freedom is my baby's tit in my palm, a song in the sweetback sling of her legs, the snakeoil slide of dreadnaught guitar standing hard in darkened dayroom corners. freedom lurches in and out of my life heavy as the swollen secret of a noose.

home

my mother once laid down with her hips and ground my globe down to this: mantle of head, hair and skin to tell the story of a boy. 23 years of texas heat and a caddo woman's midnight hoodoo hurled me away from home.

and now, five years, fifty acres, and one felon later, mother looks at me and wonders: was it whiskey, manacles, or murder that anviled my mouth into this, a gunshot of gravel pitchin' 12 iron bars of mojo.

somewhere, i traded in my fingers for a handful of fists. and there is no excuse for how my eyes, twin leather wrinkled buzzards, measure the world's weight from pussy to policy number the way a coroner's knife frees the dead's last secrets.

i am home with the hound dog's howl still running wild between the barbed wire in my head, and sleep only visits when the oil lamp shines through the night like a prisoner's dreams.

sit down and let me tell you mama,
'bout the worry iron wrought on a man.

loving era

how do i explain it? i come home with my fat curved guitar holding the voices of all the women from juke to juke, and somehow, this woman tastes through my gin and whiskey smile to find honey suckle kiss of whores on my lips. seizes the neck of my stella, smashes the give and bend of her body to floor. the room pinwheels strong as a fully swung black annie belt. hell tilts up the floorboards. balance is pushed blind into a riot of broken string and slatted wood, all my women's notes spreading their ochre and indigo to texas dawn.

and now this rock. that is my fist. that is my living. that is my hand. that blurs against her temple, a black to brown hammerfall that nails her skull into scream. this is how we love. this is the song she teaches me each time i wander back to her door.

era washington on leadbelly's stella

i got no regrets for smashing stella.
i'd beat her broke again,
rip the chords out her throat,
stomp her gut 'til it splinters
and splits all the women trapped
like meat inside the grind
he gave her hips.

i'd destroy that bitch again
to feel her throat snap
in my fist, hips smash
against my knees. see,
i thought i heard her beg
one last useless time,
carcass spilling 'cross the floor
before his fist came
down like a falling star.
but all i heard was
a guitar suck
its wire teeth,
roll its eyes
as i fell into
black-eyed
sleep.

black girl, black girl...

mary on martha...

let me tell you the difference
between me and sister martha.

when the dead get buried
beneath stone and stench
i'll give them my tithe
of tears and sweat, do my time
in the land of grief, then leave;
askin' jesus to give them peace.

martha, she'll try to change
the unchangeable, stay beside a body
beggin' god to give it a second chance
to breathe like a man.

he was a casketful of tune
that made danger look like duty.
the swampland songster wanted
to swallow the world and spit out a rind,
to flood our skulls with the weight
of loss left coiling in his soul.
and if you weren't careful
he made you want to be in his song;
fill the gap between his breaths,
the space between his hands
blooming with guitar.
made you want to forget
he was tryin' to dig his way
out of his own grave.

and see, that's where martha and me split ways.
'cause when that gallows pole/death letter

blues was mudslidin' out his mouth,
i knew enough to get out the way,
watch from my safe distance of common sense.

it was all i could do to pray for my sister
each night she traveled back to the jook,
tell her to beware of that black snake
moan. it was all i could do.

martha promise: grown summer

it was 18 and unlocking
the secret potion of bare calf and bra
strap, sheer stocking and switch.
it was knowing
heat, how a woman can bend
a man back into her heat
and knowing that fire
can burn you alive.
it was the season of knowing
and unknowing, of myth
made flesh made muscle
made music made song.

the myth snatched women up
in thunderstorms of bare bulb
back porch blues. slid beneath
shimmied skirts. pulled down
every drop of home training,
threw motherwit out the window
onto the street to stagger home.

a thin haze of rumor thickened
'round these daughters till they became
the lesson behind the need
for closed legs and bible class, the reason
for straight lace and sunday school:

you seen what happened to her, right?
you seen where the devil done reached
up and pulled her straight on down?
you seen?

i was a girl once, and then i was grown,
unfolding the difference between
what you know and what you hear.
and when i passed those fallen souls in town,
when they shared the pew in church,
i would study close their hands, their eyes,
look for the broken places in their soul.
all i could see was a godforsaken
shine still burning from their lips,
a knowledge hotter than all my mother's prayers.

will you take this load...

he came at sundown, naked
of guitar, stripped of metal slide
ring, his fingers fretless and
filled with dirty sheets.

said he wanted to know how come
i never danced much at the jook,
why i just sat there in the back
next to the door, riding a slow nod,
the silent wound in his womb of music
he couldn't quite fill with flatted thirds.

asked me to wash his seed stained, lipsticked
sheets bright clean like sunday morning
sermon so he could lay down hard
in religion and wake up to rapture.
then he lean close as summer heat:

what you know 'bout that word girl?
you know what rapture mean?

martha promise: what i knew

mama said:
don't take no truck with murderers,
but i knew the distance between
mama's worry and the swayin' fever of jook
was measured by the time it took to slip
under moonlight to fannin street's frenzy.

the blizzard of chords bustin'
through pine boarded walls
was all blood red and cider sweet:
fruit from a tree gone crazy with blues.
and when the door slid itself wide,

there he was, god's angry heel dug into dirt.
he beat that guitar like it was holdin' back
a secret lover's name; thrashed
that timber and wire siren 'til it trembled
its twelve string confessions
into the smoke ringed crowd.

yes, i knew he was married.
that his woman waited at home
while the women rode him
inch by inch, gut by gut,
grinding a way into their
common religion.

i knew what those women wanted–
all bone and gristle, the sweetmeat
of serenade he slung across their backs,
all come alive with spit and teardrop,
the magic potion of gandy
growlin' in his dance.

but i didn't know about time.
how a prison eats it up and spits a
bloodier, older man back
in your face. how it builds a wall up
and tears another one down
in the skin you want to call home.

yes, i was standing at the bottom

mooringsport moan

The trouble with the Negro started when he, while in an intoxicated condition, was disrespectful to a Salvation Army meeting that was in progress on a Mooringsport street.
                             —*Shreveport Journal,* Jan. 16, 1930

the band of whites wanted their songs virginal, full of salvation they would army on its skin like the whip marks burned into my back. but i knew the back door way of that tune, how it snuck its way out of the parlor and spread its legs wide in saloon. i sang it back to them low down and bent up, the slow, somber way you tell a man the truth about his wife, where he can really find her when he's working his hands till they're brittle as hay.

the nigger danced, bucked shadow into our music that stood up and sassed, a maddog grinding with no grace at all. moved carnal into the flower of our euphony, screwed the sun shut behind metal door of his grunt. smashed a rut of rhythm into his wrists. painted it juke. fisted fingerpop into air, flung jungle sweat from black cap of kink.

the nigger sang. a bright red obscenity grew wings around his lips, started a slow dry hump across our hymns. when we moved to scrape him from the pillar of our song, his fist sprouted shining buck blade, his grin twisted itself into a buck dance sun, and we orbited, intent on making darkness hurt.

look how easy freedom smokes from my hand when my fist starts to throttle the grip of my shank, when i teach my blade the difference between white hot air and white man's flesh.

leadbelly in angola prison: down again

this place sucks men firmly in her mouth, swallows them whole and leaves them shrunken masses of muscle. melts them down in a cast iron gut and shits them out with new names. smilin' johnny lee is now dicklicker, james baker became ironhead, joe simms makes himself rat, and roy from brazos county was beaten into tight eye.

they put me in the belly of a place with a name that lifts your tongue to the roof of your mouth with promise, *an.*.. presses back down and tells you to *go*, just as your lips beg the kiss of surprise, an *oh* that grabs liver and squeezes bowels shut. *la* pushes the dirt of truth beneath myth's fertile topsoil.

someone said this place has a faraway sound, like the songs we sung before the church and jesus lashed us down to this moaners' bench of religion. i say don't nothing sound more american than angola.

leadbelly sings to his #1 crew

Gonna jump

down,

spin

around,

pick

a bale

of cotton,

gotta jump up to go down in the bottom land, a brown bird of sweat strapped to a sack of feathered stone. gotta tumble down to the basement of hell after i done lifted up to heaven and the steel toed angels kicked me back under the sun's bright red sickle drippin' with dawn spinnin' in a sky so so dizzy with heat 'til it spills its weight on my back and wraps its blistered arms around my neck pulls down 'til i pick 500 pounds of dirty cloud from prisoned-up farm i mean 1 ton a week i mean 52 tons a year i mean bale after bale cause it ain't no bail i mean what could i make if i had bail and all the bales i ever picked? *10,000 handkerchiefs to dry my mama's tears. 20 years of double breasted suits to glide home in every day. a new tie for every time i strut through a feelgood woman's smile. a fresh tablecloth for every homemade meal i missed. and if i took a scrap from every denim and linen and dyed piece of cloth that got spun from them bales, could i patchwork a shroud wide enough, heavy enough, bright enough, dark enough, mended and torn and mended enough to lay this place to rest? and what if i set that shroud on fire?*

Gonna jump

down,

spin

around,

pick

a bale a day.

gonna? got to. can't say no. can't walk away. got to jump in. jump for the sun. jump against sky. jump across pain. jump up when i'm beat down by the riverside, where my sword and shield is my song and my word and my breath and my mama spun me around and slapped me down when i lied and stole and if only i'da listened to my mama i wouldn't be in the shape i'm in hangin' round the whiskey still and drunk on gin is what i picked is what got me here pickin' my way through this handtostalk to bolltobag to handtostalk to bolltobag to reachtotwist to plucktostuff to reachtotwist to plucktostuff a blizzard of casket-sized bales heavy enough to outweigh me and all i've ever owned, big enough to coffin up the boy i was before a pistol flash made me man, that schoolboy smotherin' in the soft strangle of cotton that i heave up from soil every day

Oh Lawdy,

pick a bale of cotton

Oh Lawdy,

pick a bale

a day…

oh lawdy jesus god did you ever carry a cotton sack i mean did you ever feel the bud in the palm of your hand i mean did you ever lift a bale like you lifted that cross jesus and did it weigh as much as a cotton field and when you show me the holes in your hands and feet can i show you the blisters in my hands and feet and can we size up the lashes on our backs and when you fell in the sun in the dust in the thorns did they wipe your face and did they look at the cloth and see my face scorched in the cotton of their cloth and was my mouth wide open my eyes squinted up from singing this song every every every every every every…

july, 1933: leadbelly receives lomax
at angola prison

the ghost of a traveler comes to my cell, carrying machinery of wire and coil, needle stuck into spinning plate of oil. tells me that this machine will stitch my stories into its black tar grooves if i hoist all i know of caddo, fannin street, the .32 and black women's hands, hurl it into song. he wants the aphrodisiac of a hundred thousand slave songs running fevers through my chorus, he wants the secret of cockwalk in the chords.

with two months left in my sentence, i twist the 12 screws that line stella's head so i can howl in double dropped D, the key that lemon always said unlocks the grave's trapdoor and drags the devil up from his harem to shiver between the strings.

i cram all seven stolen years of clearcut timber in my right hand. swing down on the strings with enough weight to buckle a man beneath knuckle and nightmare, enough to hold a head mouth down deep in baptismal waters till breath is a bludgeoned stranger. downstroke is a shotgun stock shoved hard in a shirker's back, but when my pick hits the chords on the way up, the minor chord flutters up like ravens ghosting across cane fields. my foot obeys rhythm's duty to slice the time i am serving into a metronome of teardrops.

one day, i ran to tell my father of the minstrel toy i craved. the crazed full moon of eye shone over a crescent of watermelon grin, and all it took was a twist in his back to set arms and legs in motion, grinding out a tune from tiny tin banjo in his lap. father searched my face for something he had not known as lost until then. took me out back to our fields and pulled up a palm full of earth:

you won't be nobody's slave, long as you have this.

all the time, our world sifting slow between his fingers.

out

on daddy's farm, the stallions we snared and stormed into dirt would rear high to stuff their mouths with sun, buck to kick stars out of sky. rope and spur seared servitude's lesson through muscle and bone 'til they broke beneath brand. sometimes, i would stoop far and slow in front of them, low enough to squint up into fence crazed eyes and make it plain: i would smolder there 'til beast learned to labor with man on its back or 'til we whispered for the twelve gauge shout of slavery's leaden psalm through its brain.

orphaned, swollen with texas roadside dust, i sit here counting broken years between youth's lapping tongue and the cellblock's crushing fifteen year kiss. i am a cinder on the prairie, bruise on the horizon purpling sundown's sky. i push prison's gunmetal bit from between teeth, spit sun from my head to see straight, wipe hope's stardust from heel before loading each shackle scar into my gunnysack of voice. this is how i cipher my way home, stumble my way back to a shreveport woman's arms.

home again

after it's birthed you whole and fucked you dry. after it's straddled, rode, and stolen your sense. after your fist has swung brute magic through bone and then bloomed fingers wide for caress. after you've nearly killed it and gladly killed for it. after it's cunted you down and kicked you in the cold.

after you've left it   tear dropped   tongue   torn.   after you've heaved up and hollered the sunrise and sea salt of its name 'til your throat is a hurricane of want—before and after all of this, the body of woman stands waiting.

and if you are lucky, she steps slow to the screen door of a shotgun shack and eases your rambling inside. if you are lucky, you find the hard and soft parts of yourself, blued, crumpled, crying in her hands.

martha promise receives leadbelly, 1935

when your man comes home from prison,
when he comes back like the wound
and you are the stitch,
when he comes back with pennies in his pocket
and prayer fresh on his lips,
you got to wash him down first.

you got to have the wildweed and treebark boiled
and calmed, waiting for his skin like a shining baptism
back into what he was before gun barrels and bars
chewed their claim in his hide and spit him
stumbling backwards into screaming sunlight.

you got to scrub loose the jailtime fingersmears
from ashy skin, lather down the cuffmarks
from ankle and wrist, rinse solitary's stench loose
from his hair, scrape curse and confession
from the welted and the smooth,
the hard and the soft,
the furrowed and the lax.

you got to hold tight that shadrach's face
between your palms, take crease and lid
and lip and brow and rinse slow with river water,
and when he opens his eyes
you tell him calm and sure
how a woman birthed him
back whole again.

martha promise: keeping peace

i knew about him and his hands,
how he could rip down the wall
between heaven and hate.

so, i told him about promise,
the name my daddy gave me.
how it means *make good.*
pay back on what's due.

and when i told him
about mama's cocked twelve gauge,
a warning for the first and last time
daddy crushed his hands into fists,
well, i laughed on it.
made it simple,
but not too easy.

i waited awhile, watched.
let him think on what he got,
what he could lose.
how to keep sweet
from spoilin' into sour.

yes, the music we had
was a healin' kind,
but sometimes you need a bad note
to remind you how good
harmony feels.

and so, one night,
when he was all
bent and burnt,

his palms stingin'
to slap sense into
the world,
i stared him up,
long and slow.

told him
how a man

got to sleep

sometime.

man plowing with mules

John Lomax's Recording Machine, 1933

350 lbs. of metal mockingbird,
hostage in the hold of a beat up ford,
i jerk across time's dark ocean of heat
until the trunk's starless sky flies up
and gospel white hands
lift my microphone tongue
to brown faces blistered
with the weight of song.

a hempstead woman
gently peels the sugar of her lover's kiss
from the salt of his last good-bye,
spoon feeds me her homemade tonic of loss
in the honeyed space between a cappella breaths.

a galveston guitar man breaks open
the battered wooden box in his throat,
spits a broken farmer's boll weevil fury
between my vacuum tube teeth.

a procession of paupers,
royal only in their mud
colored castles of skin,
ladles hand-me-down stories
down my copper wire throat.
each one scratches a tune from their lungs
for me to sculpt into the black world of groove
twisting galactic, slow, beneath
my shuddering diamond nerve.

Ethnographer John Lomax
Speaks of His Vocation

This country needs a Columbus like me.
I have sighted a dark territory
to map, mount, and measure: its fat, prickly
fruit weighed for value and veracity.

I stake my claim on the breath of each Black
willing to open his mouth and spit out
southern legend's soiled roots. I will blue
the pale ears of Ivy League lecture halls

with secrets snatched from between Negro jaws.
They seek the primitive man's oracle,
covet my careful codification
of these ethereal chants born from strife,

the way I pen it down in black on white
page and bid it dance; the feral language
of a folk bent and broken as the notes
grinding up through marrow and memory.

John Lomax: I Work With Negroes

I have been asked: Why did you choose to work
with the Negro? Call me librarian-
in-the-stacks-of-almost-lost-melody.
I journey this colossal, quaking book

they've authored in the space between their legs,
over blind fool hearts, beneath stomping feet,
in the liquid engine of their crooned breath.
and sometimes, the splintered edges of voice

root me in their tree of singing sunlight,
take me back to something that doesn't have
a name; our buried sense, a burning we lost
along the way to civilization.

John Lomax: On Seeking Song

To free jailed song, you need Time's wry locksmith
leaning against the con's tin can safes of sound
until they crack wide open. They've nothing
more than time in prison. Worlds of lost chance

stacked over burled heads; anger's thumb bending
caged men double 'til they spill into song.
I drive through those iron gates seeking truth
and step into a living museum,

a whetstone where the slave song just won't stop
sharpening its teeth, carving each chorus
from cell after cell of toiling human
ruin. A dying music's last refuge.

John Lomax Visits Leadbelly
in Angola Prison: July, 1933

This Orpheus. He storms Hades' steel walls
wielding notes wept by birch and spruce. Guitar
spreads her hips over his, sings of mercy,
coaxes his bottlenecked fingers to slide

the knowing into light; the dead face down
into dust to find their sorry way home.
He smolders into a growl that stops short
this side of kill, folds into shuddering

welts, and smashes through Satan's warped mirrors
screwed tight inside men's minds. Hurt's avalanche
scrapes my skin loose from sense. This primeval
archive...this heart thunder lost in a well

of whispers...this voice of smoke riddled sheen
hauling mojo up from hell, chord by chord...

He sang me a song which I shall copy-
right as soon as I get to Washington
and try to market in sheet music form.

leadbelly's role:
March of Time Newsreel No. 2, 1935

ANNOUNCER: To the Louisiana State Penitentiary goes John A. Lomax,
Library of Congress curator, collector of American folksongs.
LOMAX: Just one more, Leadbelly! (Leadbelly plays a tune in his cell)
LEAD: Thank you, sir, boss. I sure hope you send Gov. O.K. Allen
a record of that song that I made up about him, 'cause I believe he'll turn me loose!

in this movie i play the minstrel,
the shadowbox shuffle on the silver screen
shining between king kong and tarzan.
i play myself. jailtime, crimes, 49 years,
and brown's bad luck make a monster
of mangled-up dream, a demon that throws
its rusty leg 'cross my back, hooks its fingers
in the crooks of my jaw, riding me into this grin
that i ride into the scalding camera light,
ghostin' myself through the window
of a black and white picture factory,
a house of reeling shadow that stares me dead
in the face, the light burning me into fame,
shadow folding me into memory.

this hat in my hand that fits like a nail
on every nappy head, that fits in my palms
like a child's begging bowl; this beg i borrowed
from a sharecropper's scrawny harvest
to shine my way out the devil's lockbox,
to shine my way past my skin,
to shine my way into their leathered hearts;
this bossman chant's thick, purple fingers

shoving down my throat, draggin' out a hearse
full of living through my teeth;
this thanks—stolen from inside a prayer
that got ransacked 'soon as it wandered
outside my mama's mouth:
i want to remember the moment when it all got so familiar,
how i got used to the words taking over my skin,
how i taught my knees to bend without my back talking back,
how i told my head to bow when the time was right,
how please squeezes out my eyes faster than my mouth
can swallow the reasons why.

i want to know if jonah ever rode
the belly of a whale like mine.

*LEAD: Thank you sir, boss, thank you! I'll drive you all over the
United States and I'll sing all my songs for you. You be my big boss
and I'll be your man. Thank you, sir, thank you, sir!*

leadbelly: mythology

This man has been the recipient of wide publicity in various magazines
of national circulation, ~~the story usually being~~ that he sang or wrote
such moving appeals to the Governor that he was pardoned.
~~Such statements have no basis in fact.~~
He received ~~no~~ clemency,
~~and his discharge was a routine matter~~
under the
~~good time~~
law
~~which applies to all first and second offenders.~~
~~L.A. Jones, Warden, Angola Prison~~

five year sentence

For one dollar and other valuable considerations, including the services of Alan Lomax, I hereby agree that the division of the net receipts from musical engagements during said term above expenses shall be one third to me and two thirds to John A. Lomax.

when you reach for the pen,
you know there's no balm
for bad luck's bitter herb,
so you close your eyes and pray. no,
you close your eyes to blink it back. no,
you breathe in the last breath of a man
who knew his value in weight and work,
blink hard, let out the air of a man who knows
the difference between way and no way out.

you pick up the pen slow,
the ginger, bloody way your knees
kissed concrete for your last crawl
out of sugarland prison solitary.

you pick up the pen
the way you lifted your shovel
to bury a blizzard of convict coded bodies,
the state's cipher covering names
with the sound of loose earth hitting coffin lids.
#45902, #52642, #82365, on, on, on,
a gospel–bent blues beneath each number,
but when you add them all up
they equal the same: another man dead
after sun and soil and stripes and sweat

stole everything he ever had
and willed you to bend your back
around yet another spade.

you pick up the pen, and when you put it down again
you are two thirds less than what you started with.
one third the man your father raised you to be.
33 cents on the dollar for each time you open
your circle of song to push blues
into a circus cage spotlight
that shrinks as tight
and as small
as your skin.

leadbelly's labor on the lomax trail, 1934

i strain against starvation
as i climb into lomax's ford,
grinning like a fresh batch of please,
on my way to my first new job
in my latest patch of freedom:
to coax song from prisoner's
prayers. to convince the convicted
of righteousness stuck stinging
in their throats.

sugarland, angola, parchman:
when i walk in, the grave opens up,
sweat box and cinder-block
boiling their way inside
'til my brain is a jig of jail-
bird dream, the light sucked
so hard from my marrow
'til even brother shadow
got more spark than me.

when they gather 'round
i hammer out the tune,
hook the cons with a chorus of steel,
baiting their mouths open
till they sway, tattered with the notion
of a humble hobo jesus
holdin' steady this line to glory.

prisoner #489235, parchman farm, mississippi september 3, 1934

My Dearest Della

averything is ~~good~~ fine down here
How is it over there?
i did not get a leter
from last month ~~again~~
but i no you is busy with the baby
an a year is one long time. so you
rite me when you can.

time don't way no lesser tho.
we got to hunch it up at sunrise cause
when thay says go you got to go
an then you keep on till the sun hidin
an then maby som mor
after that.   but do not worry
Baby it will be allrit. four mor
years an then i be home. in time.

last week thay brung in these
travlin mens. a old White man
an his driver was a jailbird niger
like us calld Ledbelly.
seem like wen that driver singed
it was all of us in one mouth.
we got real qiet then.

they had a box that spred your voys
on a black platter and serve it up

hot an hissin in your face.
i singed them that pea pickin song
we used to sing in the garden
and wen i singed it was like
i culd smell the dirt we used to own.
i wish you culd here it Della.
we culd sing togather again.

well got to go now.
you take care of yoursef and
please kiss our son for me.
i am thinking of you allways.

your Husband
Jack.

the song speaks

an ex-con finds me
when he's statue still,
"thinkin' with his heart,"
summoning his bones
the way a gambler whispers
luck to the die he's clenched
and hurled from his palm.

a professor embalms me
in electrified wax,
then exhumes me at 78 rpm
with needle and wire,
tattooing my breath–
less body into wind.

whether i was born in the soil
or from the heat of muscle
against soil, from body-bent
trees or the river they all drink
from; whether i pass down
from callus or calumny,
goddamn or gospel,
my birthing way
is always the same.

i heave memory,
want, and will
against lung until
the soul's meat
surrenders, makes way
for the knee-buckle
load mined

from each moaner's
private graveyard
of chance.

sticky with god,
i shove and smooth
my way up gullet,
hauling treasure
chest of fingerpop
and footstomp.
i mount the skull:
starward-tilted,
open-mouthed,
praying my name
as if i were its own
into the book of heaven.

you don't know my mind...

LEAD BELLY:
BAD NIGGER MAKES GOOD MINSTREL

John Lomax: Have you got a pistol?
Leadbelly: No sir, I got a knife.
John Lomax: Lemme see it. What do you do with that thing?

★★★

The easiest way to avoid

thieves? this knife serves to bottleneck

or at least to mitigate

and stare down would-be cheats from

the consequences of sin

scheme and scam; to make them fear

is to entertain

how a blade can slice—

your fellowman.

stab through low moan—

Amuse the public,

then feast to the hilt

and you can get away

with rank murder; to cleave,

with almost any crime.

to split magic from mean.

Prime example of the great

blues is a hard, muddied sound,

humanitarian

and packed to the flesh with

appreciation of

an ex-con's shaking nerve:

criminal talent is the case of

strings bent to a higher power like

Huddie Ledbetter,

a telegraph line

better known as Lead Belly.

sendin' death letters back home.

leadbelly v. lomax:
song hunting, 1934

for every tune and chorus
we've caught in our spinning net
the bloodier twins run loose,
burnt sweet ugly with revenge

with every new recording
we've freed music from flesh. but
the lower, darker versions
could escape our microphone.

what won't get heard reeks of our payback.
jingles of ground glass poison,
ring-shouts of joy for splendor
-sent heart attacks, dirge ballads
of spooked horses throwing bossmen
hollers cradling shotgun shells—
all that crimson stuffed so far
down our tunnels of throat to
where it forgets its true colors
on the way up, bends itself blue

a brutal magic, hidden, unsung:
break-downs that set backs buckling,
gospel shouts to save angel
from the devil, melodies
from the cloudy heights of power,
blasting a way beyond pain,
into the womb of blood-song,
that place of smoked azure hope,
of ebony and tan and black
as mississippi midnight tides:

these are the songs that won't give themselves up.
they know the difference between truth and hurt;
between what white folks say they want,
and the lie they really want to hear.
these wounds we hide mostly
beneath jim-crow skin.

songs of revenge get crushed by lynch-rope fear.
anger's coffled fists reach hard, deep inside,
shove their brutal weight to twist truth
so we can deny our whip-lined will...
buried in the marrow

John Lomax writes home, 1934

Leadbelly is
        a nigger
to the core
of his being…

He is a killer.

He tells the truth
only accidentally…

He is as

        sensual

as   a goat,

and when he sings

to me

my spine

        tingles…

sometimes

        tears

                come.

Penitentiary
wardens all tell me
I set no value on my life
in using him as
traveling companion.
Don't be uneasy.
He thinks I freed him.

I am bringing him

to New York.

leadbelly writes home, 1934

martha:

lomax is carpetbagger
to the core.
truth slides itself
slicked up and sideways
out his mouth,
dressed up in the way
he wants to see the world.

so i let him brag on
how "he freed me"
'cause the fastest way
to a white man's heart
is through his lies,
the fastest way out
of his grace
is truth.

leadbelly v. lomax
at the
modern language association conference, 1934

a costume. an outfit.
dark overalls, new blue jeans,
handkerchief, clean head wrap,
and ugly-ass shitkickers, some simple, old, sturdy shoes
clutched like gifts in his outstretched hands are a proper field hand's uniform,
chase the stink of mule dirt back down-on-the-farm-familiar:
into my head. now he wants me dressing down—it raises gods
to wrap my music in a brown bag of coon dark enough to capture the authentic blues,
to give them *what folks 'spect to see,* bringing southland to a crowd that
says i need the genuine look of farm boy says they want to hear how it sounds for a black
to sow blues' dirty fingers between their ears to scrape heaven's dusty starlight out of hell.

i remember to tally up
fame's promises: and close accounts—
$100 suits is what made me believe. $3 for the coveralls, and they were on sale.
$50 wing tips made me a convert. $1 for the work boots, sold at half-price,
$5 cigars helped seal the deal. and here, a handshake serves as contract.

like always, it's strange, but,
dog-tongued anger sometimes loathing
laps at my palms, bursts from his eyes,
shrinks my bowels pummeling me—
like a clenched fist striking 'cross my face

let's face it

i'm parole on parade, i'm an ex-con's keeper,
wanted poster on a short leash, something I can't much forget
biding time beneath the law in this prison choked country—
of a master i chose myself. i cannot absolve this man of
that faded rucksack of *yassuh* his greatest crime—the crime of race—
growing one load heavier binding us all to blood,
with each slow grin cutting through skin,
stitched across my lips burning through history.

lomax v. leadbelly
in new york:
letters to home, 1934

i am disturbed and distressed at   this man messin' with my music,
his beginning to show off   preachin' how a songster gotta be pure
in his songs and talk   —like he got a deed to folkways,
when his money value is   the way blues sweats out a man
to be   like prayer
natural and sincere   set free from smotherin'
as he was while in prison: in a solitary cell.

of course,   fact is,
as this tendency grows,   this two time jailbird loser—
he will lose his charm   he ain't 'bout to lose nerve, too,
and become only an
ordinary,   old timey,
low ordinary   busted out,
harlem   countrified
nigger.

lomax v. leadbelly:
on the road, 1935

...i had made only a few requests of him, there was some things i was prayin' he'd do
and those for his protection —things to keep peace while
in a strange country; travelin' together:
i wanted him to quit botherin' on where
to eat good food, and what's healthy, and
to take plenty of rest, risin' with the sun, and
not to sing and play no midnight parties
for groups of negroes at no jook joints
late at night, until dawn.
and not to drink —lord knows, it was
too much.

lomax v. leadbelly: dreams

my dream

of setting up

in life wasn't his—

him and

his small "dream"—

martha on a farm

with this simple negro

stocked with cattle, pigs, chicken

livin' like a domestic

etcetera,

and such—livin' small

with a room in the house unlocked

for his pleasure, grinnin' up

only when

"de big boss and de little boss"

come to visit—

wantin' our shine: yeah—

was only

white folk's fantasy,

a

fake

dream.

good morning babe, how do you do?

leadbelly & martha:
return to new york, 1936

i'll unload the trunk, air out the best suit

    i empty the bags, hang our jackets loose

up on the closet rod. the south is past,

    as shreveport shakes out of our boots and hats

and so we sweep our small room one more time,

    to make room for the light of neon signs

wiping walls with hard new harlem shadows

    that flicker in the stoplight's red/green glow.

guitar filled palms and washerwoman hands

    good luck, steady work—all we got that can

hold back a landlord's eviction note—

    keep us fed on brittle scraps of hope—

that's all we need. 'leastwise for tonight.

    a clean start, a place to make things right.

jimmy goodwin, age 9

Dear Grandma

I hope that you are fine Grandma we miss you
up here where it gets cold and I miss that sweet
potato pie you made last time you visitd.
You know how the naybors here is all cramed up
on each other not like when I visit in Virgina.
You can hear them all threw the walls.

Daddy says our naybors is real cuntry folk
I lisen to them threw the wall befor I go to sleep
and they sing something sound like rain
most the time but sometime it sound like thunder to
and sometime it sound like First Missionary Baptist
Church when the preacher is saveing souls.

I seen the naybor walking up the stairs with his gitar
one day and he was mean looking but then he called me
little man and I was laghing. he sound like he got heavy hands
becus sometime when hes playin he play to loud
and daddy hav to pound the wall.

But one time he playd and daddy stoped and lookd like far
away and mama stoped to. I think they wer smiling,
but they might have been frowning to that is what I think.
I askd daddy what was wrong and he lookd
like that time Granddad went away.
he didnt say nothing. He akts like that somtime.
See that is why you shud come and see us this summer
becus I think we need that sweet pie you make Grandma.

Grandma when will you visit us
you know we miss you!

XXOXX

Jimmy

leadbelly's big city hustle

a clean start. a place to make things right

as prayer and cool as fifty dollar bills

fresh in my palm when i stroke stella high–

up and down-low, 'til the crowd gets all still:

that's all i wanna reap from this concrete farm

where they call the jook joint a cabaret

and folks burrow underground in subway cars.

even there, a busker can pull good pay

between the thunder rush of metal

that crashes under 42nd street–

damn if it don't ring my head like a cymbal…

but the green i earn can keep our feet

in shoes that we plant beneath our bed

after strummin' till the sky bleeds orange-red.

brownie and leadbelly:
stipulations and apprenticeship

There were certain stipulations —some rules I would endure:
lead wanted bluesmen dressed proper,
and I didn't like wearin' suits that
want to be high-class—to
live
up to them old traditions:

Your necktie on, nails all buffed—
Your shoes shined clean as church.
You didn't carry your guitar on your back, can't tote your stella like a hobo sack,
you carried it in a case. cradle her in lush velvet.
You don't take your coat off onstage bear a suit stern as a preacher's collar—but
Lead was always
beautiful
Neat as a pin,
and clean
as a brand new bottle

martha: life's work

after strummin' til the sky bleeds orange, red-

eyed and raw-throated lead stumbles on home

and warms up the cold space on our mattress.

we touch slow for a small while, before

i rise to the mountain of laundry and lye

that every cleaning woman got to climb

without a stop, without gettin' no higher

than a washtub bottom or maybe the tile

i bend my knees into every day

in park avenue apartment buildings.

this is how we keep a living. we pay

on lay-away with spent muscle, stealing

back our flesh between the twilight and sunrise

so we can own one thing what's got no price.

To: Haywood Patterson #386j49

Condemned Department
Kilby Prison
Montgomery, Ala.

Dear Haywood,

I am writing you from New York City. A long ways
away, I know. But I write to let you know—Negroes
and Whites alike have not forgotten you in the
dungeon. I have just left a benefit concert here that
was well attended and well spirited as well.
The Holy Father has blessed us with this at least.

There were many speakers and musicians there, one
was a Negro who had commited much more evil
crimes than the one they have falsely claimed you for.
And can you beleive he sang him self out of the Texas
prison? Begging the warden for pardon!

I wish I could carry whatever he got in that voice of
his that broke him out of jail, wish I could fold it up
and seal it in this letter, mail it to you, his simple plea
for pardon that would be your level call for justice.

Do not give up. Justice shall be ours. Since you was
taken along with my son, all of you Scottsboro boys is
my son. We will not let them forget.

You take this dollar and use it well. It is all I can send
now and we will send you more later. Trust in the
Lord, son.

Mrs. T. Montgomery
New York City,
August 13, 1937

leadbelly: one thing

so—we might own one thing what's got no price

in new york city besides dirty air,

roaches, and mice: besides this voice i try

to work into song with every spare

night: 'sides martha's hands, scrubbin' and bleachin'

'til her palms turn leather, her feet can't stand.

see, with all that sweatin', we keep our reason

posted in the front of our minds: can't

never fall back to shotgun shacks no more.

sharecroppin' dreams die in northern cities—

got to make new plans for the winter cold,

or that heat bill gone steal the shelves empty.

no, we ain't livin' on striver's row, 'though

we hustle just like them fancy negroes.

John Lomax writes home, 1937

Here I am, back in Sugarland to reap
what the law and history have sown.
These songsters ripen in captivity–
I have picked one, named Iron Head Baker,

who will be under contract to me.
Lent him from Governor Allred, freed
on special parole. Less disappointing
that way. One foul word and he'll be packing,

back to where he crafted those sorrow songs.
Unfortunate, but if Lead taught me nothin'–
he taught me caution. I dragged him into history,
and look at my thanks. *I still remember him,*

an arrogant person, dressed in fancy clothes–
a self-confident boaster. Poor Martha!
Poor Leadbelly! What the future holds
for these two Negroes, only time will tell.

martha: weight

we hustle just like them fancy negroes,

them new-found bourgeoisie. but they don't hold

to no old-time reels or sukey jumps: no,

they wanna leave them songs behind, throw

em' back downriver to slowly drown

in the mud, or fill a southern cousin's mouth.

sometimes, though, they color sneaks on out

when lead floats em all the way down home. how

quick they do remember when the feelin'

hits em' square upside the heart. they ain't dead

to the rhythm of a worksong peelin'

scabs from old wounds. they just want to forget—

to lighten up so they don't suffocate. seems

ol' leadbelly songs pull too much weight.

josh white writes home, 1941

Dear Sis,

Here is my latest disc:
The Harlem Blues.
It's all about comin'
from the South
and payin' Northern dues.
Scratch a Harlemite
and you'll find Carolina,
Mississippi, Atlanta, Virginia—
you choose! All up here
in 30 square blocks.

There's good music to be heard
here, too. I've met quite a few
songsters and reelers and those
that can wail better than most.
We meet in the clubs, or when
this Texan, Leadbelly, and his
wife Martha play host.

I met a pair here named McGhee and Terry,
a rough one named Lightnin'
and even the good Reverend Gary
from Laurens rolled through.
Got some white folks, too—
one Okie named Woody
and a college boy, Pete.

Learned a few things
from that old Texan, though.
He takes a song slow,
then winds it up hard,
sometimes too raw
for these city folks.
They like their voices
with a bit more velvet touch—
you got to woo them with a croon
before you give em' a punch.

You'll hear that on this record,
I hope. Send me a note when
you get this. And tell Mama
I love her. Give her a kiss!

Yours, Josh

cab calloway on leadbelly

ol' leadbelly songs? pull too much. eight

will pull you down, friend. and this world too fast

not to be flyin.' ain't no doubt he's great

on that guitar, and back in the past,

around '35 i'da hired him quick—

but he was stuck on that plantation shit,

playin' for nickels and dimes each gig.

it was a sucker's game and boy, he bit.

can't rake in tall cash with that country sound,

and all that small-time livin' brought him low—

last i hear he's worn himself to the ground.

them old time reelers, they go down slow

and ragged, howlin' life raw like a blues song

'til fever's run cold. till' the last breath's gone.

stella: diminuendo

my lover grows old.
his grip starts to fade
so he takes on new ways,
works his hands slower
'round my waist—
don't really thrash no more,
just strums his hands
'cross my belly,
might croon a song
'bout "workin' his jelly."
i'll whisper along,
and i wonder on
how long it's been,
all this travelin'
from road to road to road.
worth every step, though.
worth every nick and scar,
i'd guess. come this far
mostly through sweatin'
and starving' and whatever
else you'd call love.
yes, it's been too much
and then too heavy,
and then too little.
and enough.

martha: vigil

'til fever's run cold, 'til the last breath's gone

i'll stand here wiping down his brow.

a few more hours till we see the dawn

together. such a small, bright thing. right now

it's the one gift we got left. no more high

songs or low blues. them hands can't hold guitar,

keep a beat. that red river voice 'bout dried

to its rocky bed. my lead: *look how far*

we been, baby. ook how far we come. yes,

it's been some travelin'. sometimes crooked

backroads, sometimes straight ahead.

this one last morning, lord, then i'm alone—

on my way home to do what widows do:

i'll unload the trunk, air out the best suit.

leadbelly: christened

captain stared down like always—
i watched his boots mark the dirt.
he spat his juice on my nap of skull,

laughed, and bore this ledbetter
to leadbelly in one breath's pull.
i was born there, in the dusk,

after i'd dogged my crew down rows
till the bolls were bloody with our work.
king of the twelve string? no. joker of air:

took everything i ever owned, spread it
hot between heaven and dirt
till it bust out the jaws of children

swollen by this country hurt.
they'll spit my voice out from deep in
and you'll find me branded

in their skin, in a tongue
my mama dug from earth
and planted in my head.

here i am. tumbled
in the prison, swept
by the river,

bent by the burden,
swallowed in the gut,
branded by the crime,

lifted by the music
in my blood,
in my memory,

in my name.

Notes

Section titles are taken from titles of Leadbelly's recorded songs.

page 69, John Lomax Visits Leadbelly in Angola Prison: July, 1933: Italicized portion is from John Lomax's letter to Ruby Terril, 1933.

page 70, leadbelly's role: March of Time, Newsreel No. 2, 1935: Italicized text is excerpted from the "March of Time" newsreel, February 1935, as performed by Lomax and Leadbelly.

Page 72, leadbelly: mythology: The poem is an erasure of a letter from L. A. Jones to Irving Halpern, Chief Probation Officer, Court of General Sessions, New York City, 1939.

Page 73, five year sentence: The epigram is taken from the Supplement to the contract between J. Lomax and H. Ledbetter dated February 9, 1935.

Page 83, Lead Belly: Bad Nigger Makes Good Minstrel: The epigram is taken from the March of Time newsreel, February, 1935. The poem's title and italicized text are from *Life* magazine, April, 1937, page 38.

Page 85, John Lomax writes home, 1934: Excerpted from Lomax's letter to his wife, 1935.

Page 89, lomax v. leadbelly in new york: letters to home, 1934: Italicized text from John Lomax's letter to his wife, January 1935.

Page 90, lomax v. leadbelly: on the road, 1935: Italicized text from John Lomax's *Negro Folk Songs as Sung by Leadbelly.*

Page 91, lomax v. leadbelly: dreams: Italicized text from John Lomax's *Negro Folk Songs as Sung by Leadbelly.*

Page 98, brownie and leadbelly: stipulations and apprenticeship: Italicized text from interview between Charles Wolfe and Brownie McGhee in *The Life and Legend of Leadbelly,* page 228.

Page 102, John Lomax writes home, 1937: Italicized text from John Lomax's *Negro Folk Songs as Sung by Leadbelly.*

Leadbelly's Timeline

1888 – Huddie Ledbetter born in Caddo County, Louisiana to Sallie and John Wesley Ledbetter.

1902 – Father gives Huddie his first pistol, a Protection Special.

1903 – Father gives Huddie his first guitar.

1904 – Moves to Fannin Street in Shreveport, LA.
Future wife Martha Promise and her twin sister Mary are born.

1906–8 Travels west, tours with his guitar.

1908 – Marries Aletha Anderson (Lethe).
Works in cotton fields of Dallas, TX.

1912 – Studies and plays with Blind Lemon Jefferson.

1915 – Arrested for assault.
30 day sentence to Harrison Co. chain gang.

1916 – Escapes to Bowie Co., assumes alias "Walter Boyd."

1917 – Kills Will Stafford in a fight over a local woman, Chammie.

1918 – Sentenced to Shaw State Prison Farm for 5 – 20 years.
Makes two escape attempts. Drowns a hound dog during his last attempt.
Gets his nickname "Leadbelly" through dedication as a work squad leader.

1920 – Transfer to Central State Prison Farm, "Sugarland."
Last of parents' land sold for legal fees.
John Ledbetter dies.

1924 – Sings for Texas Gov. Pat Neff, asks for pardon.
Released by special order of Neff.
Begins relationship with Era Washington, common law wife.
Meets Martha Promise.

1930 – Stabs Dick Elliot in Mooringsport, LA; sentenced to prison.

1933 – John Lomax meets and records Leadbelly in Angola Prison.

1934 – Released from prison due to "double good time" behavior.
Solicits and receives work from Lomax.
Joins Lomax on the road, collecting songs.

1935 – Marries Martha Promise in New York.
Splits with Lomax, returns to Shreveport with Martha.
Threatens to sue Lomax over copyrights pending release of *Negro Folk Songs*,
and wins a settlement.

1936 – Ledbetters return to New York.
Negro Folk Songs As Sung by Lead Belly, "king of the twelve-string guitar players of the world," longtime convict of the penitentiaries of Texas and Louisiana, edited by Lomax, is released by Macmillan Publishing Company.

1937 – Records various tunes, including "Bourgeois Blues" and "Scottsboro Boys."

1939–	Arrested for felonious assault and is sentenced to eight months on Riker's Island.
1940–	FBI surveillance of Ledbetter begins due to his relationship with Communist Party. Recording contracts with several labels including RCA, Victor, and Atlantic.
1949–	December 6: Huddie Ledbetter dies at the age of 60 in Bellevue Hospital, New York City, of Amyotrophic Lateral Sclerosis (Lou Gehrig's Disease). He is buried at Shiloh Missionary Baptist Church between Mooringsport and Longwood, Louisiana. A formal memorial was dedicated on his grave in 1993.
1950–	Oct. 16: "Good Night Irene," as recorded by The Weavers, is rated #1 for 13 weeks on the Billboard charts. It is played 1,400 times per minute by 2,853 radio stations, 99 TV stations and 400,000 jukeboxes across America.

References

Filene, Benjamin, *Romancing the Folk: Public Memory and American Roots Music.* University of North Carolina Press: Chapel Hill, North Carolina, 2000.

Killeen, Sean, ed., *Leadbelly Letter.* Lead Belly Society: Ithaca, New York, 1990-98.

Lead Belly: Bad Nigger Makes Good Minstrel. Life Magazine. Time Inc.: New York, New York, April, 1936.

Lomax, John A., *Adventures of a Ballad Hunter.* The Macmillan Company: New York, New York, 1947.

Lomax, John A., John A. Lomax Family Papers. Center for American History, University of Texas: Austin.

Lomax, John A. and Lomax, Alan, ed., *Negro Folk Songs As Sung by Lead Belly, "king of the twelve-string guitar players of the world," longtime convict of the penitentiaries of Texas and Louisiana.* The Macmillan Company: New York, New York, 1936.

Porterfield, Nolan, *Last Cavalier: The Life and Times of John A. Lomax, 1867-1948.* University of Illinois Press: Urbana, Illinois, 1996.

Ramsey Jr., Frederic, *Leadbelly: A Great Long Time* by Pete Seeger. Serpent & Eagle Press: New York, New York, 1982.

Wolfe, Charles and Lornell, Kip, *The Life and Legend of Leadbelly.* HarperCollins: New York, New York, 1992.

Acknowledgments

The following poems have been published in various publications:

580 Split: "leadbelly sings to his #1 crew," "leadbelly vs. lomax: song hunting," and "LEAD BELLY: BAD NIGGER MAKES GOOD MINSTREL"

Black Renaissance Noir: "leadbelly's lessons," "sallie ledbetter: a mother's hymn," "john wesley ledbetter," and "fannin street signifies"

Brilliant Corners: "five year sentence"

Callaloo: "leadbelly v. lomax in new york: letters to home, 1934," "prisoner #489235: parchman farm, mississippi, september 3, 1934"

Cave Canem Tenth Anniversary Anthology: "bud russel, prison transfer man"

Fishousepoems.org: "leadbelly v. lomax at the modern language association conference, 1934," "1912: blind lemon jefferson explaining to leadbelly"

Indiana Review: "leadbelly in angola prison: down again"

Mid-American Review: "lomax v. leadbelly: on the road," "leadbelly: christened," "John Lomax Visits Leadbelly in Angola Prison: July, 1933," "july, 1933: leadbelly receives lomax at angola prison," "stella: diminuendo," "John Lomax's Recording Machine, 1933," "Lomax: I Work With Negroes," "home again," "loving era," "era washington on leadbelly's stella," "Ethnographer John Lomax Speaks of His Vocation," "lomax v. leadbelly: dreams"

Ninth Letter: "home," "will you take this load...," and "martha promise: what i knew"

Obsidian III: "caddo born," "blind lemon taught me," "for trouble's sake," "leadbelly: runagate," "leadbelly: from sugarland," "sing out," and "Governor Pat Neff"

Ploughshares: "freedom" and "out"

Web Del Sol/Perihelion: "harris county chain gang," "home again," and "martha promise receives leadbelly, 1935"

Believers...

Without so many, this book would not have been. My mother, Della McGraw, who believed and believed and believes. Brother Gordon, a shoulder to lean on. Sister Paula's inspiring tenacity. My father Jesse and his many books. This would have been an unimaginable journey without the Cave Canem workshop, those who gave me a home to build my words, especially Cornelius Eady, Toi Derricotte, and Carolyn Micklem. Camille Dungy, with clear, brass vision. Elizabeth Alexander, a great convincer. Sterling Plumpp, who tended the spark. Afaa Weaver for the fire. Tim Seibles, Nicky Finney for the flame. Keli Stewart, who gave light. So many fellow travellers: Quraysh Ali, Duriel Harris, Regie Gibson, Joel Dias Porter, Brandon Johnson, Major Jackson, Honoree Jeffers, Toni Lightfoot, Van Jordan, and Vivee Francis— the living definitions of generous camaraderie. The Callaloo Workshop, with the watchfulness of Charles Rowell, the eyes of Reetika Vazirani. The Green Mill/National Poetry Slam and Mark Smith with loud outspokenness. The NYU crew, especially Melissa Hammerle, Russel C., Sharon Olds, Galway Kinnell, Philip Levine, Marie Howe, and Tom Sleigh—they helped me work it on out. Provincetown's Fine Arts Work Center gave airy space. Chicago's Guild Complex gave community. Ragdale Foundation gave respite. Illinois Arts Council came to the rescue. The NEA came through in the nick of time. Brigit Pegeen Kelly, who gave it a chance. Tiny Robinson, who continues Leadbelly's legacy. Many others along the way…

Tyehimba Jess' first book of poetry, *leadbelly*, is a winner of the 2004 National Poetry Series. Jess received a Literature Fellowship from the National Endowment for the Arts in 2004 and was a 2004–5 Winter Fellow at the Provincetown Fine Arts Work Center. He won the 2001 Gwendolyn Brooks Open Mic Poetry Award, an Illinois Arts Council Artist Fellowship in Poetry for 2000–2001, and the 2001 Chicago *Sun-Times* Poetry Award. He was on the 2000 and 2001 Chicago Green Mill Slam teams and is also a proud Cave Canem alumnus.